Responding to
Student Writers

Responding to Student Writers

Nancy Sommers
Harvard University

Bedford / St. Martin's
Boston ◆ New York

Manufactured in the United States of America.

7   6   5   4   3   2

f   e   d   c   b   a

For information, write: Bedford/St. Martin's, 75 Arlington Street, Boston, MA 02116   (617-399-4000)

ISBN 978-1-4576-1934-2

Acknowledgments

Cover photo: Mara Weible.
page 26: *Hilda* cartoon. Copyright © Phil and Stacy Frank.
page 37: *Amanda and Her Cousin Amy, North Carolina, 1990.* Copyright © Mary Ellen Mark.
page 38: *St. Jacques Gypsy Boy on New Year's Eve.* Copyright © Jesco Denzel/VISUM.

Contents

Note to fellow teachers

Responding to Student Writers is a modest book, written from one fellow teacher to another, to remind us of the many ways in which responding extends the work of the classroom and helps students become critical readers of their own words. Responses to student writers come in many forms—written or spoken comments on rough or final drafts, for example, or e-mail messages or discussion posts responding to specific queries about thesis sentences or research proposals. Responses to student writers also come from many sources—from teachers, from classroom peers, and from writing center tutors. I have chosen to focus this book primarily on the teacher-student relationship and on written comments, but the strategies in this book apply to both written and oral comments and extend to peer response, too.

And I have chosen to write a practical book to offer some common-sense strategies for setting the scene in the classroom, engaging students in a dialogue about their drafts, writing marginal and end comments, and managing the paper load. I hope that we can continue to share strategies, stories, and suggestions on the book's companion Web site, hackerhandbooks.com/responding.

Fellow composition teacher Howard Tinberg reviewed the manuscript for this book in its early stages and pointed out that strategies for responding to student writers are "needed more than ever." He also pointed out that we are teaching more and more students, in the name of productivity and efficiency, and asked, "How do faculty who are committed to the teaching of writing continue to assign papers knowing the tremendous work required?" Responding does indeed involve tremendous work, but the relationship between a teacher's comments and a student's learning cannot be underestimated. What this book offers is one teacher's view of how the ways in which we respond to our students as writers, and the dialogues that we engage in across drafts, help students develop as confident academic writers.

Acknowledgments

A book of this kind is a long time in the making and draws on the talents of a wide range of teachers, students, colleagues, and family members. It is a pleasure to acknowledge the abundant contributions of so many people without whom this book would never have been written. I am indebted to my own teachers who patiently struggled through the dense fog of my drafts, responding and inspiring, and showing me the power of thoughtful commentary. And I am grateful to my students, who, over many years, received my comments with grace and goodwill.

A wonderful group of colleagues, near and far, have discussed and debated the ideas in this book, and took me to task when they knew I was wrongheaded. In particular, I would like to thank David Bartholomae, Pat Bellanca, Jean Ferguson Carr, Pat Kain, Suzanne Lane, Eric LeMay, Les Perelman, Sondra Perl, Maxine Rodburg, Laura Saltz, Mimi Schwartz, Sallie Sharp, Dawn Skorczewski, and Pat Spacks. And to Kerry Walk, I offer deep thanks for our years of sustaining conversations about teaching writing and our lively exchanges about responding. I am also grateful to many scholars in the field of composition and rhetoric who have written so intelligently about the topic of teacher commentary and enriched my thinking: Chris Anson, Richard Beach, Lil Brannon, Peter Elbow, Rich Haswell, Cy Knoblauch, Melanie Lee, Ronald Lunsford, Carol Rutz, Jeff Sommers, Richard Straub, Ed White, and Kathleen Blake Yancey.

Many of the core ideas in this book grew out of talks I've given at conferences and arose from workshops I have led at more than one hundred colleges and universities. I am grateful to the talented faculty, graduate students, and writing center tutors who challenged my thinking, widened my perspective, and encouraged me to write this book. In particular, I would like to thank the Bunker Hill Community College Writing Program, especially Professors Tim McLaughlin and Jennifer Rosser, for their suggestion to add one more piece to this project—to see teacher commentary through students' eyes—and their invitation to interview their students.

A wonderful group of readers and reviewers generously offered their own ideas on responding, pushed me to expand my thinking, and provided creative suggestions. I would like to thank Jill Dahlman, Jill Darley-Vanis, Dana DelGeorge, Karen Gardiner, Stephanie Knoll, Jill Kronstadt, Mark Merritt, and Howard Tinberg. And thanks to members of my writing groups—Ann Bookman, Sandi Morgen, Carol Stack, William Hagen, and Jeff Meyersohn—for offering their generous critiques. And I want to acknowledge and express thanks for the important contributions of Katie Becher, Bob Cummings, Anne-Marie Hall, Amy Kimme-Hea, Noreen Lape, and Albert Rouzie to this project.

My Bedford/St. Martin's colleagues have been faithful friends throughout this project. Joan Feinberg, president of Macmillan Higher Education, envisioned a role for this book long before it was written. Michelle Clark, executive editor, guided this project from its early stages, encouraging its development, responding with her keen, intelligent editorial eye, and cheering me onward throughout the writing process. A writer can't ask for a more thoughtful and treasured editor than Michelle. Many thanks to Mara Weible, Barbara Flanagan, and Kylie Paul for their assistance and editorial support to improve the readability of my prose—and to Denise Wydra, Karen Henry, and Jimmy Fleming for their support and friendship. I am grateful, too, to acknowledge the help of Rosemary Jaffe, Laura Winstead, Linda McLatchie, and Claire Seng-Niemoeller for their design and production expertise.

Finally, I extend thanks to my family for their abundant love and generous support, always needed and much appreciated. My daughters, Rachel and Alexandra, grew up doing their homework at the kitchen table, writing their compositions while I responded to those of my students, believing that's what moms do—they read student writing. And many thanks to Josh for reading each chapter multiple times, cooking and baking and keeping our home humming while I disappeared to write. And to my extended family—Alexander, Brian, Charles Mary, Curran, Demian, Devin, Kate, Liz, Ron, Sam—many thanks for offering wit and wisdom along the way.

This book is dedicated to my mother and father, Walter and Louise Sommers, and my aunt, Elsie Adler, who encouraged me to write and set me forth on a career of writing and teaching.

Nancy Sommers

Introduction

> The writing teachers' ministry is not just to the words, but to the person
> who wrote the words.　　　　　　　　　　　　　　—William Zinsser

I have been a teacher of writing for more than thirty years—it's work that
I love, especially teaching first-year students. By now, I've read more than
ten thousand drafts, probably more drafts than anyone is supposed to read
in a lifetime. Reading drafts—and responding to student writers—takes up
more time, thought, empathy, and energy than any other aspect of teaching
writing. We feel a weighty responsibility when we respond to our students'
words, knowing that we, too, have received comments that have given us
hope—and sometimes despair—about our abilities as writers. The words
teachers wrote on our papers, inscribed in memory, are often the same
words we scribble in the margins or at the bottom of our own students'
pages. We hope that our students will learn from our comments and will
carry those words forward as they move from our class to the next, from one
assignment to another, and across the drafts. We don't take this responsibility lightly. The work of entering into our students' minds and composing
humane, thoughtful, even inspiring responses is serious business.

Responding *is* serious business—and seriously time-consuming. A truth
not often acknowledged about teaching writing is that we actually spend
more time with students' drafts than with our students. The amount of time
we spend in the classroom, even preparing for the classroom, pales in com-
parison to the enormous time we spend in reading our students' drafts. Like
most teachers, I have rituals when approaching drafts: lots of coffee and
plenty of cookies; sudden desires to cook, try new recipes, clean and rear-
range closets, or check e-mail and return phone calls—anything to distract
and comfort during the nights and weekends devoted to a tall stack of papers.

If teaching involves leaps of faith, responding is one of the greatest
leaps because we have so little direct evidence of what students actually do
with our comments, of why they find some useful and others not. Responding consumes so much time and energy, and yet, paradoxically, it is the element of our work that we least understand. If, for instance, you asked why
my students choose to use some comments and ignore others, I would have
to say that *I just don't know*. Of course, I hope that I haven't overwhelmed
them with too many questions or directives or written anything perplexing
or discouraging. And I hope they take my comments to heart in the same
spirit with which I have written them. But I often feel that the loneliest

moment in teaching writing comes when we return papers. I've learned not to return drafts at the beginning of class—otherwise, there goes the class—but after spending long nights and weekends with students' drafts, I watch students walk out of the classroom, sometimes glancing at my comments, but most often not. I wonder if these comments will go unread and unused, and I wonder what happens between drafts, between the moments when drafts are handed back and when students submit their revisions.

Why comments matter

Though I know little about the actual process of how students read and respond to comments, or why some students are grateful for copious comments while others are disappointed, I know that written responses are the most enduring form of communication we have with our students. As responders, we dramatize the presence of a reader, reminding students that their writing is actually intended for a reader and for a particular purpose. As one student told me, "It must be tough looking at a very large stack of papers, but it is the most helpful part of the writing process because without a reader the whole process is diminished." Yes, *without* a reader "the whole process is diminished," and *with* a thoughtful reader the entire process is enriched and deepened. For first-year students, teacher commentary is their most personal, most direct interaction with the college writing culture, and the relationship between teachers' written responses and student learning cannot be underestimated. Our comments also play an important social role: They help students feel less anonymous and convey a sense of academic belonging. As my colleague Kerry Walk observed, "Comments do such hard work, no wonder we have to work so hard to produce them."

We comment on students' writing not only to demonstrate the presence of a reader but also to help our students become that questioning reader themselves, because ultimately we believe that becoming such a reader will help them read and respond to their own thoughts and words and develop control over their writing. And we comment on their drafts to create a motive for revising: Without comments from teachers or peers, students might assume that their drafts are finished, complete, and ready to be abandoned. When students receive comments telling them they have "great insights," or that their teachers have "never seen the topic discussed this way before," or that there might be "a whole level of deeper questions" for them to imagine, students understand that their teachers view them as people with things to say, as thinkers capable of insight and depth. Or when teachers ask students to revise their thinking, it is not just the teachers' words students hear and carry with them across the drafts; it is also the teachers' belief that they are independent thinkers capable of doing good work, even if as first-year students they are not yet accomplishing it. When students respond to their teachers' constructive comments and revise their ideas, they do so because students imagine their teachers as readers waiting for their ideas, not as readers waiting to record what they've done wrong. Knowing that there is a real, live person—a teacher as reader—at the end of the composing process imbues that process with meaning and significance that would otherwise be absent.

Considering a writer's development

Too often both teachers and students feel overwhelmed by the process of giving and receiving comments. Teachers feel overwhelmed as they try to *fix* every problem in a draft, believing that their job requires them to comment on each compositional element and that pointing out such errors will prevent students from repeating them. And students feel overwhelmed by the sheer number of comments and the bewildering hieroglyphics scribbled on their pages—dots, check marks or question marks, squiggly or straight lines, even the compositional shorthand of *Awk* and *Frag*. Students are often unsure whether these comments are meant as observations, suggestions, requests, pleadings, or commands, especially when they receive contradictory directions to fix commas in sentences that in fact need to be rethought—in essence, to both proofread and develop—making it difficult for students to decide what is most important and what is least important. From a teacher's point of view, however, it is difficult to withhold corrections when there are so many surface-level problems in usage, diction, tense, and style, and our lack of restraint makes it easy to blur the distinctions between revising and proofreading.

Still, if we recognize the slow pace of writing development—that is, how long it takes to learn *how* to write a college paper, to have something to say to a reader who wants to hear it—we become rather humble about the enterprise of commenting. Writing development is painstakingly slow because academic writing is not a mother tongue; its conventions require instruction and practice, years of imitation and experimentation in rehearsing other people's arguments before being able to articulate our own. The movement from novice to expert looks like one step forward, one step back, one compositional element mastered while other elements fall away. If comments play a role in writing development by moving students forward as writers, they do so because they teach *one* lesson at a time, resonating with some aspect of writing that students are already thinking about. The whole enterprise of commenting becomes more interesting and less overwhelming when we ask ourselves: What *single* lesson do I want to convey to students through comments? And how will my comments teach this lesson?

Seeing comments through students' eyes

From 1997 to 2001, my colleagues and I followed four hundred students from the Harvard class of 2001 through their undergraduate years to explore the role of writing in undergraduate education.[1] The collection of more than six hundred pounds of student writing and five hundred hours of taped interviews gave us an opportunity to witness the wide range of comments that students receive, not just in one course or from one teacher but over four years and across academic disciplines. To see comments through college students' eyes is a kaleidoscopic experience: papers returned with no responses, just a grade; papers returned with bewildering hieroglyphics; and papers returned with responses that treat students like apprentices, engaging with their ideas, seriously and thoughtfully. What emerged in every conversation with students about their college writing is the power of comments, their presence or absence, to shape writing. When students were asked each year to describe their best writing experiences, two overriding characteristics emerged: (1) the opportunity to write about something that matters to the student and (2) the opportunity to engage with an instructor through written comments. What became clear from students' testimonials is that teachers' comments play a much larger role than we might expect from scribbled words in the margins or at the end of a draft. Implicitly or explicitly, these words contain messages about who students are and who they might become as writers, and they reveal teachers' investment in their students' potential. These messages can propel students forward with their writing, inspire them to experiment, and provide a reason to master the conventions and expectations of academic writing.

One college senior, reflecting on the role of feedback in his undergraduate writing career, told me: "If I bumped into one of my professors twenty years from now, I would know what this professor thought of my work; our minds connected at this juncture of my paper, and I will always be indebted." The word *indebted* caught me off guard. Indebtedness, after all, carries with it a connotation of obligation, of being beholden. But indebtedness also carries with it a feeling of appreciation and gratitude, a legacy of connectedness. From the students we followed, I learned that comments need not be monumental, but their influence often extends beyond the margins of student papers and outside classroom walls.

The call-and-response of commenting

My own thinking about the purpose of responding has been influenced by one of the students in the longitudinal study who offered the following provocative comment: "Too many teachers' comments are written to the paper, not to the student." At first, this simple distinction seemed puzzling; after

[1] I am grateful to the research associates of the Harvard Study of Undergraduate Writing—Laura Saltz, Kerry Walk, Suzanne Lane, Pat Kain, Soo La Kim, and Emily O'Brien—for their dedication and energy throughout the four years of following four hundred students.

all, when sitting alone with a stack of student papers, we are sitting with our students' writing, not with the students who wrote these words.

If we write comments directed to the person who wrote the words, rather than to the words themselves, what would these comments look and sound like? To start this new practice, I began by asking: If a student were sitting beside me, how would I approach the process of commenting? Would I begin, as I sometimes do with my written comments, by delivering a lengthy monologue to tell her what is deficient and missing in her paper, as if there were an ideal paper and hers has come up short? And would I tell her not to worry about her paper's shortcomings because they will be fixed and corrected by her teacher's directives? I hope not.

Everything shifts when we transfer the focus of our comments from the paper to the student, from monologue to dialogue, and from teacher-centered commands to teacher-student partnerships. As with any partnership, each partner has a role in this exchange: Our role as teachers is to engage with students by treating them as apprentices, offering honest critique paired with instruction; and for students, it is to be open to the teacher's comments, reading and hearing these responses not as personal attacks or as isolated moments but as instructive and portable lessons to take with them to the next draft or assignment. This partnership has as much to do with students' willingness to hear and accept honest and constructive assessment of their work as it does with teachers' willingness to offer such an assessment. Everything shifts, as well, when we realize that the language of our comments derives from the relationship forged with our students in the classroom and forms part of that classroom conversation, rather than a separate language for response, with separate customs, conventions, and hieroglyphics. Since we sit alone with our students' papers, engrossed in our own rituals of response, we may forget that responding begins in the classroom, on the very first day of class, not at the moment when we assume joint ownership of our students' drafts by taking up residence in the margins or at the foot of their papers.

Most writing teachers don't choose their profession to become comma cops or grammar guardians. Most find their calling in the back-and-forth of the classroom, the call-and-response between student and teacher, and in the deep pleasures of nurturing students as thinkers, readers, and writers. Sometimes, though, when teachers separate responding from classroom work, they forget that comments are an extension of the many voices in our classroom, not just their own. And sometimes teachers may forget that their responses need not be monumental; they need only answer students' basic question: *How do I write a good college paper?*

Setting the scene for responding

Responding to student writers is a conversation that begins in the classroom. We would never think, for instance, of hurtling into the classroom to bark a series of commands — *Be specific! Avoid generalizations! Develop more!*; to speak in codes—*Awk, Frag, Punct*; or even to perform a series of dramatic gestures—*The exclamation point! The question mark? The squiggly line ~.* Yet the margins of students' papers are often crammed with these monologues—shorthand commands, codes, and gestures that contain messages about student-teacher relationships, whether respectful, paternalistic, or lopsided. Nor would we enter our classrooms attempting to teach every compositional lesson in a single day. And yet we often overwhelm students when we spatter our responses across their pages, employing our comments to identify their drafts' shortcomings and sending mixed messages about the processes of revising, editing, and proofreading.

When sitting alone with our students' drafts, feeling the weighty responsibility of responding, we often forget that all writing, including our comments, is written to *someone* for a specific *purpose*. In the case of responding, though, everything becomes complicated because teachers play so many different roles—reader, diagnostician, coach, gatekeeper, judge—and we use our comments for multiple purposes of teaching and learning. This chapter looks at the implicit and explicit messages of written comments, especially through the eyes and experiences of student writers, and suggests that responding becomes less overwhelming, for both students and teachers, when we focus our purpose on student learning and ask: *What will students learn from our written comments? And how will our comments teach these lessons?*

Offering one lesson at a time

Let's start with a story that is a touchstone for me, an example of almost Zen-like advice, written in a respectful tone that provided a student with a single durable, transportable lesson. As part of the longitudinal study, my colleagues and I asked seniors to look through their portfolios of college writing to identify examples of effective comments. Looking at her bulging portfolio, Mary pointed to the influential words written on her first college paper and explained:

> This paper was my best guess of what a college paper should look like, a typical five-paragraph theme about *Macbeth*. My teacher wrote comments in the margins and at the end of the paper, but one piece of advice stayed with me: *Try to do something a little less safe next time; ask a question you don't have an answer to*. I didn't quite understand what he meant, but I realized that I was being asked to try something different from my five-paragraph high school routine. So I approached my second college paper by asking a question I didn't have an answer to: Why does *Cymbeline*, a tragedy, have a happy ending? This approach was somewhat scary at first, but as I began to see how much more interesting it is to start a paper by puzzling out what I don't know, rather than starting with what I know, I found an approach to use for most of my college papers.

If we understand responding as a form of give-and-take, we might consider that the conversation begins with Mary asking: "How do I write a good college paper?" This isn't an easy question for any teacher, novice or veteran, to answer in a few words. And it demands a specific answer, not a generic one, addressed to each student's particular set of skills and disciplinary interests. I would like to imagine that Mary's teacher didn't rubber-stamp these simple words—*Try to do something a little less safe next time; ask a question you don't have an answer to*—on every student's paper, but rather wrote them to Mary to show his confidence in her, as well as his understanding of her readiness to move away from a safe high school method. His words encouraged Mary to be brave, to take a risk, to tolerate uncertainty, and to try something new. That these words guided her long after she left an introductory literature course might stem from her instructor's modest goal of teaching one doable and practical lesson at a time, as well as his belief that other lessons would follow from this one. As a first-year student, Mary wasn't asked, in the words of David Bartholomae, "to invent the university," or even to invent the field of literary criticism or composition. Instead, she was invited to learn one new and specific lesson—*ask a question you don't have an answer to*—and to take an apprentice's first step as an academic writer.

Understanding the purpose of comments

Commenting on student drafts serves multiple purposes, but the overarching purpose is to show students how to write a good paper. Too often, though, comments aren't written with a clear lesson in mind, or even a clear sense of how a student might use these comments. Let's look, for example, at some of the comments one student, Roy, received on the first draft of his first college paper:

> James Baldwin, an American novelist, ~~once~~ said "I love America   *Cite your*
> more than any other country in this world, and, exactly for this reason,   *source!*
> I insist on the right to criticize her perpetually." Baldwin speaks   *Let's hear*
> about America the way a parent speaks about her small child. Baldwin   *more of*
> *Baldwin's*
> criticizes, as any concerned and involved parent would, to nurture   *words*
> the country he loves so deeply and to help it mature. This ability to
> criticize and to voice your opinion, whether you are for or against   *Confusing.*
> *Too* America is one of the options unique to Americans. We, like Baldwin,   *Who is*
> *general.* can say whatever we like about America and our government without   *"We"?*
> *Develop*
> *with* fear of repercussions. We are children with a very unusual privilege
> *specifics.* to voice any number of negative, dissenting views about our parent
> country without ever being punished. Americans have a unique and   *Why*
> *"unique"?*
> complex relationship with our country. As a result of our unusual
> rights and privileges, we can act as both critical parents and difficult
> children.   *Confusing analogy. Is the relationship between a country*
> *and its citizens the same as a parent-child relationship?*

Much of Roy's debut as a college writer is commendable, especially his brave attempt to use an analogy, but he probably wouldn't know it from the paternalistic tone of his teacher's comments, which cast him as a wayward student writer. The teacher seems to have approached Roy's draft with a deficit model, looking for what is wrong and inadequate, and concluding that what is absent from this paragraph is more important than what it might contain. It wouldn't matter if these comments were written in red or blue ink, scribbled in pen or typed via Word's comment function; they send Roy a message that he needs to fix, patch, and correct what his teacher marked and also to rethink the substance of the paragraph's central analogy. When I asked Roy about his reaction to his instructor's comments, he replied: "I guess my teacher didn't like what I wrote." And when asked why he thought teachers comment on drafts, he surmised that "the main reason is to tell students what they've done wrong."

We have all heard the perplexed student say to us: "I don't understand how *you* want me to change this" or "Tell me what *you* want me to do." When students receive comments such as Roy's, they quickly forget their own purpose in writing and shift their attention from "This is what *I* want to say" to "This is what *you*, the teacher, are asking me to do." If we look at these comments from Roy's point of view, we can see how confusing this process must seem: Should he patch first and then develop? Or develop and then patch? The remarkable contradiction of asking Roy to edit sentences that probably won't be in a subsequent draft, especially if he develops a new analogy, suggests a confusion of purposes that only reinforces Roy's belief that teachers comment primarily to show students what they have done wrong.

The dangers of overcommenting

Research on responding confirms that overcommenting does more harm than good. Students become overwhelmed and discouraged; teachers get exhausted. Moreover, offering too many comments, especially negative ones, often gives students an inaccurate view of who they are as writers and who they might become. I imagine Roy's teacher as a dedicated and conscientious instructor with the best intentions to help students become successful college writers, but her comments are exhausting to read and most likely were exhausting to write, especially if she wrote such copious comments on each student's draft. In responding to a single paragraph, she willingly plays multiple roles—comma cop, gatekeeper, critic, and judge. She has shown Roy his mistakes and communicated that he has much to learn, but she hasn't shown him *how* her questions, commands, and pleadings will help him write a good college paper. What's more, she hasn't pointed out anything positive, anything for him to build on as he revises. It is important for Roy to see what he has accomplished in his first draft and how he might gain traction with the ideas present in this draft.

One of the major challenges of responding is that there are an infinite number of lessons we might want our comments to teach, but a finite number of lessons students can learn in writing and revising a single paper. We can understand why Roy's teacher wanted to point out the paragraph's multiple problems with commas, citations, diction, and syntax, as well as its lapses in specificity, accuracy, and clarity, but it is impossible to imagine Roy learning all of these lessons while revising his first college paper.

It is healthy to remind ourselves how daunting and complex the conventions of academic writing must look to first-year college students, even to most undergraduates, as they grasp and practice what seems, at first, a set of esoteric codes. We also need to be empathetic about our students' capacities as apprentices to absorb and learn from comments, and we need to be humble about the limited influence of any one comment. No comment, no matter how brilliant, insightful, or articulate, will be sufficient to shape a fully formed writer. Although we labor to write comments, they aren't really for us or about us. The purpose of responding is not to show students how smart or clever their teachers are, or to reinforce the hierarchy between student and teacher by correcting students' errors. Rather, the purpose of responding is to promote students' authority and authorship by giving them feedback about their strengths and limitations as writers. And the feedback loop provides a double perspective for students to see what they have learned and accomplished, as well as what they still need to learn.

Responding to rough versus final drafts

The purpose of responding to rough or early drafts differs from the purpose of responding to final drafts, and comments should be matched to the draft at hand. An early draft is a work in progress (like its student writer); its ideas are in flux and are still being formed and tested. The writers of early drafts need nurturing encouragement and honest assessment to see where they stumble and where they succeed. By contrast, comments on a final draft have a different purpose because they need both to evaluate the strengths and limitations of the current paper and to provide transportable lessons for future assignments.

For example, in commenting on an early draft, a teacher might suggest a common revision strategy: that something the student has written at the end of a draft may be more appropriate for the opening:

Sample comment on an early draft

The thesis, as stated in your first paragraph, is more a statement of fact than a debatable proposition, but your final paragraph hints at an interesting argument and possible thesis. Consider the possibility of revising your conclusion to become your introduction.

But such a comment, if written on a final draft, would confuse process with product, given that the paper is finished and that the student will be moving on to the next assignment.

Comments on final drafts need to provide transportable lessons that students can take with them across drafts and assignments, and they often contain phrases such as *For your next paper, you might want to try . . .* or *Before writing your next draft, ask yourself. . . .* For instance, in responding to a final draft, a teacher might offer the following lesson on *how* to arrive at a thesis and engage a reader with an arguable claim.

Sample comment on a final draft

When you approach your next paper, try to begin with an intriguing detail, especially one you find difficult to explain. Beginning in this manner not only draws in your reader but also forces you as a writer to grapple with a troubling aspect of the text, which can often be a key aspect that you had previously set aside. This, in turn, can focus your thesis and argument.

Such a comment on a final draft treats the student as an apprentice, an evolving writer, and provides the student with a bridge to cross to future writing assignments—*those details that you have dismissed might be more important than you first imagined; start with details because they engage readers.*

Finding the right tone

Our comments are written for specific purposes—to inspire, to encourage, to nurture, to evaluate—and are written to our students, who need respect and honesty, not harshness or mean-spiritedness. Reading many hundreds of pages of student writing collected for the longitudinal study, I was surprised by the variety of teacher commentary, some of which was written with a disrespectful edge. Tone is the essence of a comment; *how* we phrase a response is as important as *what* we say. The same comment can be phrased in different tones and often makes the difference between students feeling dismissed and insulted and students feeling respected and taken seriously. Consider, for instance, what it must feel like to receive comments such as *What you say, you say nicely, but you don't really say very much*; or *You've written a rant that makes you sound like a radio talk show host, not like a thoughtful student. Curb your opinions because nobody wants to hear them.* Ouch!

Hurling insults at the student writer who sounds like a "radio talk show host" won't turn his opinions into reasoned arguments. Our "host" needs to learn how to be open to opposing points of view and how to become a thoughtful and reasonable writer. And the student who doesn't "really say very much" needs to be shown *how* to read her own words to detect the differences between empty sentences that don't "say very much" and those sentences that communicate an idea with some depth and complexity. To develop authority as writers, students need guidance and specific advice, always phrased in an encouraging tone.

While writing this book, I had the wonderful opportunity to interview fifty students from Bunker Hill Community College about their teachers' written comments. What struck me in all my interviews was the vital role that tone plays in encouraging students to become stronger writers and, by extension, stronger students. Bunker Hill students used two words— *encouraging* and *discouraging*—to describe the tone of their teachers' comments. Encouraging comments are described by students as "gifts," given by "someone who walks with you," who says that "you're on the right path," and who is "on the same page as you."[2]

By contrast, discouraging comments leave students feeling as if something has been taken away from them, with nothing being given in return. Students describe the discouraging comments with metaphors such as "having the rug pulled from under [them]," "being shot down," or "being nailed." As one student remarked, "If you take something away from a student who isn't a strong writer, you don't leave him very much."

What I learned from seeing comments through the eyes of both Bunker Hill and Harvard students is something quite simple and comforting. Tone is the essence of a comment because it speaks of the powerful relationships created in the acts of giving and receiving responses. To college students, teachers' comments are often their most personal contact with their institution and carry messages larger than the words themselves.

---

[2] I am grateful to the faculty members of the Bunker Hill Community College Writing Program for their invitation to interview their students, especially for the generous assistance of Professors Tim McLaughlin and Jennifer Rosser.

Developing a common language

Responding begins on the first day of class, not at the moment we establish residency in the margins of our students' drafts. Just as we stride into our classrooms with assumptions about who our students seem to be, so, too, our students pick up messages, implicitly or explicitly, about their teachers' expectations, values, and dispositions. Students are confused if the persona we project in our comments is different from the person who shows up every Tuesday and Thursday to teach. They are equally confused if we use a separate language for responding, one they see for the first time in comments on their papers, a vocabulary that is unrelated to their classroom discussions and exercises. Responding is more effective when the language of our comments comes from the classroom, rather than using a separate language with separate customs and conventions. Creating a common language with students, especially one that comes *from* the class rather than one that is imposed *on* them, connects and unifies various elements—discussions, exercises, assignments, and peer and teacher comments.

Here's an example of how I connect the common language of my classroom with my comments. I define *thesis* as an essay's main point or central idea that is often formulated as (1) an answer to a question posed, (2) the resolution of a problem identified, or (3) a statement that takes a position on a debatable topic. That's a great starting point, but students can't grasp *how* to develop an engaging thesis until they repeatedly practice putting their theses to a reader's test: *So what? Who cares? Why would someone want to read an essay that explores this thesis? Would anyone disagree with this thesis? If so, what would this person say?* Throughout the semester, these are the questions my students ask themselves and their peers whenever we workshop a draft, discuss tentative theses for a given assignment, or analyze the rhetorical effectiveness of writers' theses and arguments. Commenting on their drafts, I often use some part of the familiar "So what?" language to show students how to transform their descriptive theses to argumentative theses and how to find a motive for their arguments. When students say *I don't think my thesis has a "So what?"* or when they tell their peers *There's no "So what?" to your thesis*, I know that we're all speaking the same language and that they have begun to grasp the dynamic process of crafting a thesis.

Creating a link between classroom and comments

Students often tell me that the comments they most understand and use are those that have a background or context because such responses employ the familiar language of classroom instruction—the terms and phrasings already in play between students and teachers. One of my favorite examples of a comment with a background comes from Francesco, a student I interviewed at Bunker Hill Community College. Francesco explained that his teacher used the term *spice* in class to illustrate how good academic writing always reveals a writer's personal take on a subject. As the teacher illustrated, one writer might choose oregano, another cinnamon; spice gives writing its personal seasoning, flavoring analyses and syntheses that would otherwise be bland. When Francesco's teacher wrote *Good spice* or *More spice* in the margins of his drafts, such comments functioned almost like a class within a class, taking the student back to classroom lessons about how and why writers add spice to increase their rhetorical authority.

Developing a common language with students not only brings a class together and increases opportunities for learning but also makes responding fun. In one of my writing courses, for instance, students began using the term *facing the dragon* to describe the challenge of going beyond clichés to uncover the complexity and tensions within a topic. The dragon is the difficult part of writing, often what is *not* on the page, what is lurking in the margins or at the edges of drafts and must be confronted—the more difficult or significant the topic, the more ferocious the dragon. This particular class also used terms such as *naysayer* and *worthy adversary* to acknowledge opposing points of view and the phrase *earning an ending* to describe satisfying conclusions, as opposed to forced or artificial endings. Such terms, whimsical and creative, were reinforced in classroom discussions and assignments and provided a familiar common language for comments—words to identify places in their drafts where dragons or naysayers lurked, or where conclusions remain unearned.

Establishing a common language with students provides an important method for connecting what otherwise might be disparate pedagogical components of a writing course. It doesn't really matter how the vocabulary is devised—it might be the standard language of the handbook, or phraseology created by students and teachers in the classroom. What matters most is that the words and phrases evoke a network of associations, suggest specific strategies to guide student writers, and connect the lessons of the classroom with the purpose of comments. Writing lessons don't end when students turn papers in for a grade; nor do comments begin when our words appear on students' drafts. Students are more likely to transfer their learning across the curriculum if they carry with them a common language to use when reading and responding to their own drafts.

2

Engaging students in a dialogue about their writing

Even the most thoughtful and articulate comments will have no influence on students if they don't understand how to use them. If students believe that the purpose of comments is to justify a grade or to correct their mistakes, they won't read their teachers' comments with any sense of agency or engagement. And if students encounter comments written in an unfamiliar language, they'll simply be baffled and unable to grasp the meaning. We owe it to ourselves and to our students to make sure our comments become texts worthy of reflection, interpretation, and discussion, just like every other text in the class. If papers are returned to students with no accompanying discussion about the purpose of comments, or if comments are isolated from classroom lessons, students will most likely not be able to make use of their teachers' responses. In short, students won't learn from them. To become confident and capable writers, students need to participate in a dialogue about *their* writing.

Establishing a role for students in the dialogue

Take the case of Jackson, one of the students in the longitudinal study, who, when asked as a first-year student how he might use his teacher's comments in future assignments, responded: "I don't think I can use these comments since each paper is a different assignment and a different kind of paper to work through." Jackson intuited the great challenge of college writing: to move from his first-year writing course to his courses across the disciplines — writing about Confucius in a philosophy course one semester, about a government document in a political science course the next. But on another level, Jackson's observation makes clear that it will be difficult for him to transfer comments to future writing assignments because he believes that each essay assignment is a discrete unit defined by its topic.

In Jackson's view of writing, comments are tailored to each essay but also isolated from all other essays, and their purpose is, simply, to show students how to correct their mistakes.

Part of becoming a good writer involves learning to receive and use constructive comments, both for the assignment at hand and for other assignments. Jackson is correct that an essay on Confucius is a text unto itself, but if he is to develop as a writer, he needs to understand that there is continuity from one assignment to another. Since he sees no way to transport lessons from one paper to the next, he reads his teachers' comments as isolated moments, not as bridges between assignments. Even the most insightful comments will not move students forward as writers if they believe there are no transportable lessons to be learned from their teachers' comments.

It is neither simple nor easy for students to learn how to receive and accept critique, especially how to read comments as something other than judgment on their limitations as students or on their failings as writers. While one student will respond, "My greatest reaction to all that red ink is gratitude," another first-year student will shrug and say, "I guess all these comments mean that he didn't really like my paper." Or if a student believes that the purpose of her composition course is to teach her how to "write quickly, adequately, and painlessly," we understand why such an attitude might prevent her from being open to comments that ask her to slow down, read texts closely, and, in a word, change *her* approach to writing. One of the conclusions from the longitudinal study is that a student's willingness to accept and benefit from comments, to see them as instruction and not merely as judgment, is an important predictor of college writing development.

At its best, responding extends and deepens the exchange that begins in the classroom, and it offers opportunities for students and teachers to engage in dialogue. The role of the student in this exchange is to be open to a teacher's comments, reading and hearing comments not as personal attacks or as the teacher's idiosyncrasies but rather as instructive words to carry to the next draft or assignment. And the role of the teacher in this exchange is to welcome students into the process by engaging with their ideas, respectfully and thoughtfully, treating students as apprentices, with much to gain and much to give.

If students such as Jackson believe the purpose of comments is to show them what they've done wrong, they will have great difficulty using these comments to re-see or re-envision (in a word, *revise*) their drafts. If students think of revising in terms of correcting, proofreading, polishing, fixing, and patching, they will not understand the structural demolition and renovation that are often needed between drafts. A truth not often acknowledged about teaching writing is that revised drafts aren't always better drafts. Many revised drafts are actually weaker than the original rough drafts or so similar in style and content that it isn't clear that anything has changed. Revising may (or may not) guarantee change, but it doesn't guarantee improvement. It is impossible to engage students in a dialogue about their writing if they don't grasp the purpose of comments or if they don't understand how to use these responses when revising.

Revising with comments

Over the years, I've found it useful to assume that (1) first-year students haven't had much experience with deep, global revising; and (2) I am wasting my time and theirs if I don't treat comments—both my own and those from peers—as texts to be studied and discussed. It is difficult to engage students in a dialogue about their writing if they don't understand *how* to read and respond to their teachers' or peers' comments. Thus, when we discuss revising, I use former students' drafts, complete with marginal and end comments, and in class we consider ways in which the writers of these drafts chose to use or ignore various comments. Such an exercise provides opportunities to discuss global revising—thesis, evidence, or structure—and is an easy way to talk about the purpose and style of the comments they'll receive.

Two other exercises are extremely useful for showing students how to revise with comments:

- Ask students to read through your comments or those they've received from their peers and then to write a one-page revision plan in which they explain what they learned from these comments, as well as how they plan to use the comments when revising. This interlude of reflection encourages students to think globally about their drafts, clarify any responses they might not understand, seek help from the writing center, use their handbook, and not confuse revising with copyediting.

- At various points in the term, ask students to reread and analyze your comments and to give you feedback about them. Ask students to tell you which comments are useful and why, which are not and why, and what they've learned from your comments. I've found that this exercise engages students in surprising ways—suddenly, they are the teachers—and they relish the opportunity to show instructors how their comments missed the mark. It is enormously humbling to hear students say, "You write way too many questions. What do you think I will do with all those questions in the margins?" or "You show me what I've done wrong, but you don't show me how to get better as a writer." And it is equally rewarding to hear a student discover that he or she has "started to understand how to wrestle with the evidence of a text and not to assume that evidence speaks for itself."

The Dear Reader letter

One of the most effective methods for engaging students in a dialogue about their writing is to ask them to compose a Dear Reader letter or a writer's memo to accompany their drafts. For me, this practice, more than any other, has made responding more interesting and effective: Students are reminded that they are writing *to* live readers, and they are given the opportunity to ask for specific feedback. Teachers are given an easy method for shaping their responses *to* the student writer, not to the student's draft, and for focusing their comments as specific answers to students' questions and concerns.

Although the specific instructions for the Dear Reader letter vary from assignment to assignment, I usually ask students to begin letters by identifying the strengths of their drafts. Even if I disagree with the student's evaluation, I'm given a useful way to begin my comments:

> Yes, your draft's great strength is the passion you feel for the subject, which a reader easily recognizes. One of the challenges, though, of writing about a subject such as stem cell research is that you need to remember that those who disagree with you are equally passionate about their views. As you revise, you'll want to consider these opposing viewpoints and incorporate them into your argument.

In writing such a comment, I'm trying to use a writer's strength—her passion for the subject—as a lens through which she might view what is missing from her argument—in this case, anticipating and acknowledging opposing arguments.

The prompts for the Dear Reader letter change depending on where students are in the writing process. When students are writing rough drafts, they need to ask questions about their work in progress. When they submit final drafts, they need to reflect on the differences between rough drafts and final drafts, and assess the strengths of their revision. A Dear Reader letter, like a portfolio cover letter, provides an opportunity for students to reflect on what they've learned about writing and how they plan to transfer their learning from the paper at hand to the next assignment.

A sample Dear Reader letter appears on page 13. The student was asked to respond to these prompts in his letter:

- What are the strengths of your rough draft? What are the problems of the draft?
- What were the challenges you encountered writing your draft?
- What is your thesis?
- If you had two more days to write this draft, where would you focus your attention?
- What questions are you asking about your draft that you want to make sure your readers answer?

Sample Dear Reader letter

Dear Reader:

I chose to write my paper about the death of newspapers. The strength of my draft is the relevancy of this topic. The weakness of the paper is that I assume everyone cares about newspapers. I was surprised to learn from my peer group that they read news online and think of newspapers as part of the past, not the present or the future. My challenge is to persuade my peers to care about the shift from print to online news.

If I had two more days to write this draft, I would try to develop a more interesting thesis. Right now my thesis is that the death of newspapers will have a negative effect on local politics. I would like my readers to pose some counterarguments to my thesis and tell me if my examples are effective.

Sam Jacobs

Dear Reader letters provide glimpses into students' writing processes, especially with their answers to the question "If you had two more days to write this draft, where would you focus your attention?" Students' intuitions are usually right on the mark, and they usually recognize many of the problems in their drafts, even if they don't know how to solve them. Here's how I might respond to Sam's comment about his thesis:

> One way to make your thesis more interesting to readers is to state it as a resolution of a problem you have identified or as a position you want to take in a debate. Take some time to learn more about the various debates surrounding your topic. Show your readers why they should care about the death of newspapers.

When students take the Dear Reader letter in the spirit in which it is intended, they set the dialogue in motion, and they become active partners in a conversation about their work. Feedback is rooted in the partnership between student and teacher, and, as in any relationship, it develops its own language and meaning. The exact wording of a comment is less important than what it evokes in our students and how it resonates with something they've already sensed or observed about their writing.

Making the most of comments

If students are to engage in a dialogue about their writing, they need opportunities to be full participants. And if teachers want students to read and use their comments, they need to show students how to make the most of them. When visiting colleges and universities to offer workshops on responding, I often ask faculty: "What do you want students to know about *why* and *how* you respond?" And when meeting with students and writing center tutors,

I ask: "If you could give any advice to faculty about the kind of comments you and your peers want to receive, what would you tell them?" These questions always provoke spirited and passionate conversations, as if a veil had been lifted or a long-held dark secret had been released about teachers' comments. Both students and faculty have much to say to one another; they just need an opening and an invitation to explain their perspectives.

A statement—or manifesto, as the students called it—from writing center tutors at Columbus State University to their faculty appears below.

Sample student statement about feedback

A Manifesto on Written Feedback

From the Columbus State University Writing Center Tutors

1. We would like your comments to be written to us—students. We would like you to engage us through dialogue, not through commands. We ask that you not use your comments to reinforce the hierarchy between professors and students. Instead, use comments to create a relationship with us, reader to writer, and show us that you have read our papers and care about our development as writers and thinkers.

2. We would like your comments to be specific and not generic. Point out what we've accomplished and provide specific strategies for *how* we can improve as writers. We ask that you assume that we want to become stronger writers and to learn from your comments.

3. We would like your comments to bolster our agency as writers and to deepen our thinking. We feel censored when you cross out our sentences or shut down our arguments by writing "wrong" in the margin.

4. We would like your comments to help us notice themes and patterns in our writing, rather than point out random or arbitrary mistakes.

5. We would like you to distribute rubrics with the assignment rather than at the end of the writing process. You help us improve as writers when you discuss the rubric in class, for then the rubric informs our writing process, and we can learn from it. If your rubric is formulaic and covers too many elements, it does not help us as much, for it seems to exist for you to justify your grades.

Inspired by the Columbus State writing center tutors' document, the faculty and teaching assistants in the University of Arizona Writing Program chose to craft a statement to help their students understand how to make the most of comments. The Arizona manifesto appears on page 15.

Sample instructor statement about feedback

A Manifesto on Written Feedback

From the University of Arizona Writing Faculty to Our Students

1. We would like you to understand that our comments are part of the teaching and learning process. We write comments not just to evaluate your essay, but to help you see how the writing lessons from class emerge in your writing. One way to better understand the purpose of our comments is to actively participate in class and carefully read the rubric and assignment sheet. These are the ways we communicate with you ahead of time about what we are looking for in your writing.

2. We would like you to know that we intend our comments to be constructive. We value your ideas and want to learn from you. We hope that you will use our comments to learn from us as well.

3. We would like you to approach each essay not as an independent unit, but as a brief moment in your overall development as a writer. Our comments are meant to be useful to you in this assignment and your future writing.

4. We would like you to accept responsibility for using our comments in the revision process. We also expect you to share your strengths as a writer in commenting on your peers' papers.

5. We would like you to understand that comments are both descriptive and evaluative. Writing a letter grade is perhaps the least interesting thing we do as writing instructors. Take the time to re-read the entire essay alongside our comments to understand the grade in context. We invite you to use our comments as an opportunity to talk further about your writing.

These manifestos begin conversations between students and teachers about the important role responding plays in writing development. They allow teachers—even an entire writing program—to make these ideas public, either by including them on syllabi or by posting them on a writing program Web site, and to say to students, *Here's how we comment, and why.* And such documents provide an opportunity for students to participate in a conversation about their writing, one in which they have much to gain and much to give.

3

Writing marginal comments

"I never thought I would take another music course," a student told me, "but the comments my professor wrote in the margins of my paper about Miles Davis made me believe I had something interesting to say about jazz." Although written *in* the margins, such comments are hardly *marginal*; rather, they are central to the process of learning to write. Some teachers prefer the conventional method of using pen or pencil to write in the margins of student drafts, while others prefer to type comments via Word's comment function. The method, handwriting or typing, matters less than the specific lessons conveyed to show students the strengths and limitations of their drafts.

When my colleagues and I asked students in the longitudinal study, "What advice would you give the Dean to strengthen writing instruction across the college?" we were surprised by the consistency of students' responses: Almost 87 percent of the students wanted the dean to "encourage faculty to give more detailed feedback." (By contrast, only 13 percent felt that "more writing assignments" would improve writing instruction.) Students told us, "If you don't get feedback in the margins or ends of papers, you just assume that the professor didn't read the paper or thought it was terrible." And students spoke passionately about the ways in which their teachers' comments showed them that "real readers were really reading" their words and paying attention to them.

Marginalia

Marginal comments present a record of a reader paying attention—highlighting a draft's attributes while conversing with its writer. Students don't take this convention lightly; marginal comments are the evidence that their drafts have been read closely. Without such responses, students conclude that their readers merely glanced at their words. A paper returned with no marginalia, or with nothing more than check marks and question marks scattered along the edges, suggests a breezy or distant reader. But what kind of reader do we become when we take up residence in the margins of our students' papers?

Asking myself this question, I often smile and remember a phrase used when my daughters were in elementary school: "pleasure read" — a one-hour block of time devoted each week for children, along with their teachers and the principal, to sit on the floor and read for pleasure. When I disappear to read the weekly stack of student papers, I want to say to my family: "It is pleasure read time!" But I don't, even though much of the experience is pleasurable, especially reading revised drafts. If we were reading students' papers only for the pleasure of seeing what they've done with our assignments, we would sit comfortably on the floor, savor their words, and take delight in their accomplishments and successes. But our work as responders involves reading as teachers who are ready to collaborate, to show students *how* to write good papers. And it is the *how*—how to animate a moribund thesis or how to find sufficient evidence to persuade readers—that takes time, thought, imagination, and skill.

Less is sometimes more

We need to be careful that our zeal—suggesting, commanding, or pleading how to do something differently—doesn't leave too heavy a footprint in the margins. It is easy to appropriate our students' drafts by crossing boundaries between teacher and student, between reader and writer. Here I recall a phrase from Henry James: "the brutality of good intentions." As collaborators—and I use the word with caution—our intentions are good, but our influence, unfortunately, is often brutal: We intend to show students *how* to animate a moribund thesis but end up suggesting a clever one that we find compelling; or, intending to show students *how* to find sufficient evidence, we explain why the evidence we find persuasive is the evidence they should find persuasive. In such cases, students lose their agency and passion to animate *their* theses or to seek evidence to persuade *their* readers, and the collaboration between reader and writer, between teacher and student, easily becomes lopsided, especially when students are writing about texts we've read multiple times or about topics that we, too, are passionate about. It is much more difficult to stand back and restrain our collaborative enthusiasm or knowledge about a topic, to remember that comments are written *to* and *for* students who need comments to develop *their* writerly authority.

Developing a scale of concerns

Imagine a draft's margins as the place allotted for conversational turn-taking—your turn; my turn—rather than wide-open territory that is ours to dominate. If we see the margins as territory to which we've been invited, we're less likely to be critical and ungracious, taking notice of every flaw, less likely to be the unfocused reader who offers a scattershot of random responses. And as guests, we are less likely to impose our own sensibility on a student's draft.

Before commenting in the margins, it is helpful to read the entire draft, quickly, to grasp a sense of the whole piece. Sometimes this is impossible, especially when a quick turnaround is required for a tall stack of papers. But reading an entire draft before responding often saves time; it allows us to see the arc of the paper, rather than losing our way in a draft's detours or rough patches.

In the interlude between quickly reading a draft and writing in the margins, it is important to ask: What *single* lesson do I want to convey to students? And how will my comments teach this lesson? Our marginal comments will most likely teach two or three lessons, but it is best to start with a single lesson to give students a consistent and focused response. Asking such questions helps us develop a scale of concerns appropriate for the paper we are reading and helps us avoid overcommenting. For instance, in reading a rough draft, we may confuse process and product and give students mixed messages if our marginal comments suggest that correcting spelling and punctuation errors is more important at this point in the process than identifying a clear thesis and an organizational structure to support that thesis.

Suggestions for writing marginal comments

Identify patterns — representative strengths and limitations — to help students gain control over their writing. By noticing rhetorical and grammatical patterns, we save ourselves time because we don't need to comment on every instance of the problem, especially problems that might be resolved when students focus their attention on higher-order concerns or when they proofread their papers.

A pattern may be positive: *Great job providing sufficient evidence to persuade readers*. And a pattern may highlight recurring problems: *Look closely at the ways in which you introduce each quotation to make sure you vary the language and placement of signal phrases*. By highlighting patterns, we model for students how to assess their own strengths and limitations.

Anchor marginal comments in the specifics of a text to avoid vague directives. Most teachers have a series of commands — *Be specific! Develop more!* — that they place in the margins of student drafts. Although we need some form of shorthand, these commands don't show a student *why* a paragraph would be strengthened with specific evidence or *how* to analyze evidence to develop claims. Text-specific comments demonstrate that we're reading drafts carefully, rather than rubber-stamping a set of generic comments. If, for instance, a student has asserted that "cultural differences make it difficult for Italian students to study in the United States" but has not provided support for this assertion, a teacher might comment: *What details and examples show these cultural differences? Why do these specific differences create difficulties for Italian students?* Since the purpose of comments is to teach a lesson — in this case, specificity — comments should be anchored in the specifics of students' drafts to guide their revisions.

Use the common language of the classroom to engage students in a dialogue about their writing. If we employ language that students don't understand, our comments will go unread and unused, and we have wasted our time and theirs. Students are more likely to be engaged if comments are phrased in familiar language and as questions, rather than as directives. For instance, instead of writing *Revise your vague thesis*, I might write: *How does your thesis answer the "So what?" question?* This is a shorthand way of saying: *Remember Tuesday's class when we revised thesis statements by responding to your classmates' "So what?" questions? Now it is your turn to revise your thesis by asking this question.* If such a comment engages a student, it does so by creating a coherent link between classroom lessons and their specific draft, placing the responsibility for revising and learning with the student.

Link marginal comments to specific handbook lessons. In deciding what lessons our comments will teach, we are guided by the patterns we observe in students' drafts. For instance, if we notice a pattern of sentence fragments or comma errors and we correct each error, we've become our students' copy editors. By contrast, if we identify for students one or two instances of such errors and refer students to the sections of their handbook for a fuller explanation, we respect and encourage students' abilities to self-correct and revise.

Handbooks become more useful companions for student writers when they are also a teacher's companion for responding, not only for identifying grammar errors but also for reinforcing rhetorical lessons. For instance, if a student's argument would be strengthened by including a counterargument, we might want to write: *How will someone who disagrees with your position respond? Refer to page X in your handbook on anticipating and countering objections to see how to incorporate opposing arguments.*

It is easy for teachers to feel overwhelmed by the process of writing marginal comments, especially when we try to fix compositional errors and believe it is our job to respond to every problem in each draft. I often remind myself not to comment on a problem just because I notice it; to do so is to respond to the writing, not to the writer. After all, it is not the quantity of our marginal notes, or the mistakes we catch, or even the insights we've achieved about students' drafts that matter most in students' writing development; rather, it is the capacity of our words to engage students in an exchange about their writing. Questions alone may not engage students, but questions anchored in the specifics of a student text and phrased in the common language of the classroom are more likely to create a role for students in the exchange. Our dialogue is much more likely to resonate with students if we continue to ask: *What lesson am I trying to teach?*

One of my favorite stories about responding comes from a Seinfeld routine: As Jerry Seinfeld tells it, his teacher returned a paper with one marginal comment: *Vague.* Seinfeld drew an arrow to the comment, wrote *Unclear*, and gave it back to the teacher. The teacher then handed it back to Seinfeld with another single comment: *Ambiguous.* According to Seinfeld, "We're still corresponding to this day." Although most likely apocryphal, Seinfeld's story provides a cautionary tale about the kind of exchange, easily parodied, that we don't want to foster: teachers' holding the license for vagueness while commanding students to be specific.

4

Writing end comments

Like marginal comments, end comments (also called final or summary comments) are an occasion for engaging students in a conversation about their work and are best phrased in the familiar language of the classroom. Both marginal and end comments dramatize the presence of a reader and say to students: *I have read your draft, and here is how it looks from my perspective*. Though different in format — marginal comments are often written in shorthand, whereas end comments are often written as letters—and different in purpose—marginal comments ask students to pay attention locally, whereas end comments ask students to pay attention globally—they work together to provide a consistent message about a draft's strengths and limitations.

End comments on early drafts

End comments on early drafts need to focus on specific lessons for revising. If students have been asked to identify their drafts' strengths and weaknesses in a Dear Reader letter, their reflections will guide the conversation. Students might not be the best judges of their own work, but they become better judges when they are asked to reflect and participate in the back-and-forth of responding. As teachers, our work is to help students see their words from the perspective of interested readers and to guide their re-seeing, as they separate the processes of drafting from revising, crafting from editing. Since revising requires writers to delete—what one of my students called "slash and burn"—what they've worked so hard to create, our end comments ought to acknowledge the strengths of what they've accomplished before we proceed to identify their drafts' global problems.

A sample Dear Reader letter and a teacher's end comment intended to motivate revision appear on page 22. The student, Jamal Hammond, was asked to respond to these prompts in his Dear Reader letter:

- What are the strengths of your draft?
- What is your thesis? Your argument?

- How does your thesis answer a reader's "So what?" question?
- What opposing arguments do you acknowledge?
- What was the hardest part about writing this draft?
- What questions are you asking about your draft that you want to make sure your readers answer?

Sample Dear Reader letter

Dear Reader:

The strongest part of my draft is my argument. Here's my thesis: Athletes who use any type of biotechnology give themselves an unfair advantage. My argument is that drugs should not be used under any circumstances even if they are available. The "So what?" of my thesis is something I'm still trying to figure out. I didn't have trouble thinking of an opposing argument because I know most people my age believe that athletes should be able to use performance-enhancing drugs since these drugs make it possible for athletes to perform better and break world records.

The hardest part of writing this draft was figuring out which sources to use and how to quote them. I still don't understand MLA citation.

I have two questions: Do you like my draft? Do you find it convincing?

Jamal Hammond

An instructor's end comment on an early draft

Comment [CherylYee7]: Dear Jamal:

You've written a promising draft about an important ethical issue: the role of performance-enhancing drugs in sports. You are right about the strength of your draft: A reader has no doubt about your position.

Your argument would be more convincing, though, if you didn't dismiss your opponents' arguments so quickly. (See marginal comment #5.) Try to help readers understand what distinguishes a "fair" from an "unfair" advantage and why "fairness" is more important than breaking world records.

Please see marginal comments #1–4 to help you think about how to strengthen your use of quotations. We'll be reviewing MLA in class this week.

I look forward to reading your next draft.

Sincerely,
Professor Yee

Professor Yee's response to Jamal is written in a conversational tone, allowing the writer's concerns to set the agenda, and she focuses her comments to teach key lessons about academic writing. She begins the exchange by affirming their common ground: "You are right about the strength of your draft: A reader has no doubt about your position." She shows confidence in Jamal's ability to find the missing piece of his argument and never appropriates his draft by suggesting a right answer. Likewise, she doesn't impose her view about how to make his argument more convincing, but she does offer a method: "Your argument would be more convincing, though, if you didn't dismiss your opponents' arguments so quickly."

When I asked Professor Yee why she chose to defer comments about MLA citation until a future class session, she explained: "It was early in the term, and almost all of the students were confused by MLA citation and documentation conventions. It is much more efficient to ask students to bring their handbook to class, teach the lessons again, and ask students to return to their drafts to apply what they've learned." And when I asked why she chose not to respond to his question "Do you like my draft?" she observed: "First-year students are vulnerable and just want to know if they are meeting college expectations. Jamal's question, like the questions from all students, offers a snapshot of who he is as a writer at this point in the semester. I chose to answer the second question—'Do you find it convincing?'—because that seems more important than whether I 'like' or 'dislike' his draft."

End comments on final drafts

In the example below, a history professor uses an end comment on a student's final draft to teach a single lesson.

Sample end comment on a final draft

Comment [BrianHenry4]: Dear Sonia:
A major strength of your paper is its originality. You bring in excellent evidence to support your argument, but at times you give the reader the impression that you expect the evidence to be self-evident. (See marginal comment #4.) Selecting good evidence is one side of the coin, but analyzing it for your reader is just as important; and on that front, you can go much deeper. (Marginal comments #1–3 highlight the ratio between quotation and analysis in a single paragraph.) For your next paper, focus on a deeper analysis of the evidence. Remember that your readers want to see how you interpret evidence.
I look forward to reading your next paper.

Sincerely,
Professor Henry

Professor Henry uses his end comment to teach his student, Sonia, that evidence doesn't speak for itself. The marginal and end comments work together to provide a consistent message of specific instances (illustrated in numbered marginal comments) where deeper analyses would strengthen Sonia's argument. Professor Henry uses Sonia's strength—selecting evidence—as a lens through which she can understand her paper's weakness—expecting evidence to be self-evident—and while respecting the difficulty of the task, he expresses confidence in Sonia and guides her to work from her strengths. What might otherwise sting as a critique is softened by guidance and continuity—a teacher looking forward to reading a student's future work.

Although there are no formulas for end comments on final drafts, Professor Henry organizes his comments in a productive sequence:

- **Opens with a salutation:** "Dear Sonia"
- **Highlights the paper's strengths:** "You bring in excellent evidence to support your argument"
- **Highlights the paper's weakness:** "You expect the evidence to be self-evident"
- **Links marginal comments with the end comment:** "Marginal comments #1–3 highlight the ratio between quotation and analysis in a single paragraph"
- **Provides guidance across the drafts:** "For your next paper, focus on a deeper analysis of the evidence"
- **Reinforces the writer-reader relationship:** "I look forward to reading your next paper"
- **Closes with a signature:** "Sincerely, Professor Henry"

Taking students seriously

In offering end comments from two teachers, I'm not suggesting that these responses are templates to copy. They are instructional, of course, but like all comments they are not meant to be showcased in a gallery of beautifully crafted comments, even if there were such a museum. The exact wording of any comment is less important than what it evokes in a student and the relationship it fosters. If a teacher's comment takes a student seriously—resonating with something the student has noticed, guiding without appropriating the student's way of *seeing* and *re-seeing*—the comment will transcend the draft at hand and will travel with the student across the drafts.

When interviewing students for the longitudinal study, I heard students' observations about teachers who commented too much and those who commented too little. It was rare to hear a student say that a teacher wrote just the right amount. I'm sympathetic to students' complaints because I tend to be in the overcommenting group. Getting it "just right" is a challenge, especially in an end comment, and I constantly remind myself to focus on one or two lessons in my end comments, not an entire semester's worth of lessons for one paper. My tendency to overcomment may explain my enthusiasm for the Dear Reader letter because it offers teachers an opportunity to get it "just right." With a conversational back-and-forth of letters, we are less likely to be verbose or high-handed, less likely to spew a long list of points that need to be fixed, and more likely to remember that end comments ought to be specific, not generic, and written from one writer to another.

5

Managing the paper load

Tacked on my office wall is an image of a composition teacher, Hilda, shackled to her desk, a pile of papers yet to be read. Pen poised to write something good about the paper in hand—and something equally good and inspiring about the next paper and the next in the stack—Hilda sits slumped and burdened, wondering about that panel on "minimal marking" that might have been the key to unlocking her shackles.

This image, a little frayed around the edges after all these years, reminds me of the push-and-pull of our work in responding to student writers. On the one hand, it is an intimate kind of work to enter into students' minds

Composition People

Hilda begins to think she should have
attended that panel on "minimal marking" at
last month's conference of writing teachers.

to compose humane, thoughtful, and instructive responses; on the other hand, it is work we typically do in bulk and in batches, always leaving us feeling unable to compose a sufficiently full response.

Conversations about responding always find their way to questions about the paper load. We optimistically search for new methods, such as Richard Haswell's minimal marking, as keys to unlock the ball and chain shackling us to our desks. Yet it is a simple equation: The more drafts we assign, the more students write; the more students write, the more we comment.

Focusing on student learning

The first step in handling the paper load and managing time is to keep the connection between comments and learning squarely in mind. Simply put: We waste our students' time and our own if students can't learn from our comments. For instance, a four-page draft, covered in a sea of green ink, identifying numerous problems—such as subject-verb agreement, run-on sentences, problems with paraphrasing and citing sources, and rhetorical lessons of unclear thesis and logical inconsistencies — raises questions about what is developmentally possible between drafts. Is it realistic, within one week, to imagine a student developing the necessary skills to address so many different problems? And if we become our students' copy editors, addressing all of our students' errors, what role do we expect students to play?

Throughout this book, I have suggested that a productive way to approach each draft is for teachers to ask themselves: *What single lesson do I want to convey to students through comments? And how will my comments teach this lesson?* Such questions keep the focus on student learning and force teachers to develop a scale of concerns, from global to local, to show students where to put their attention. The teacher's responsibility is not to comment on everything, to address every error, or to become students' copy editors. And, in fact, it is counterproductive for learning when students are overwhelmed by a barrage of discouraging comments.

It is a teacher's responsibility, though, to motivate and instruct, to inspire and encourage, and to offer specific, targeted advice. But how do we do so when there is so much to say to the multiple classes of students who've delivered their papers on a Thursday and expect comments returned by the following Thursday? The best response is simply *Less is more.* Teachers save time and students learn more when teachers target only a few matters in depth rather than superficially commenting on a range of problems. Admittedly, though, choosing what few matters to comment on isn't always an easy proposition, but the guidelines on page 28 have helped me focus my responses.

How to respond with a *less-is-more* approach

Connect comments to specific assignment goals. If we construct assignments to highlight specific writing goals — clear thesis, logical organization, persuasive evidence — and we structure classroom lessons toward these goals, we provide a coherent context for our comments. Since we can't comment on every rhetorical or grammatical problem in a draft, we need to let students know the expectations for a given assignment and the specific criteria used to assess their work. We are more likely to avoid a deficit model of responding — that is, looking for what is wrong in a draft — if we show students how their drafts meet specific assignment goals.

Connect comments on early drafts to global issues. Although it may be difficult to ignore numerous surface errors in early drafts, we save time by keeping our focus on global issues before local ones. If we correct punctuation errors or fix awkward sentences before a thesis or the paper's organization is in place, our comments suggest that revision is a janitorial process of fixing and cleaning. Commenting on global issues — purpose, thesis, argument, organization, evidence, and clarity of ideas — focuses students' attention on the multiple-step process of revising.

Connect comments to patterns. When we identify a draft's representative strengths and weaknesses, we don't need to comment on every instance of the problem. A pattern — *Strong transitional sentences* or *More analysis needed* — focuses students' attention on manageable chunks. Most important, though, showing students how to identify their patterns reminds them, especially when revising early drafts, that global issues take precedence over local issues.

Connect comments to students' specific questions. Asking students to submit a Dear Reader letter and participate in a dialogue about their drafts provides an easy and efficient method to offer specific, targeted advice. When students initiate the conversation, they are more engaged and willing to accept feedback. And when students ask us questions about their drafts — *Is my evidence persuasive? Are my paragraphs logically organized?* — we can save time by targeting our responses to answer students' specific concerns.

Varying the purpose of comments

One effective way to handle the paper load is by disrupting the traditional linear model, which goes something like this:

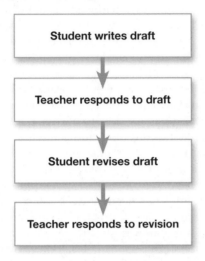

Not all drafts need teachers' full responses; not all responses need to be given to full drafts. Comments offer students instruction, but instruction comes from many sources and in many shapes and is often needed in intermediate steps between drafts. Teachers save time and students learn more when all response possibilities are creatively employed across drafts.

When confronting a semester with a heavy paper load, I ask myself: *What would provide the biggest boost to students' learning? And how might I vary and share the work of responding?* Sometimes the purpose of comments is to give a quick, targeted response to one rhetorical element in a rough draft—analysis of evidence, for example—and to engage peers in reading the full draft. Sometimes the purpose of comments is to give a specific response to a research question or a tentative thesis statement before students draft a research paper.

And sometimes I read drafts, comment lightly, and focus my efforts on developing a handout to illustrate patterns across all students' drafts. A "Trends and Patterns" handout provides an opportunity to minimize end comments, while maximizing explanations to all students about how to address and resolve common problems—meandering introductions, unfocused thesis statements, or incorrect citations, for instance. By using examples from their own writing to illustrate these patterns, students see their comments as both more universal—they aren't alone in having written an unfocused thesis statement—and more personal—they now have a deeper understanding of the purpose of comments and multiple strategies for doing something different in *their* next draft.

Varying the style of comments

A tall stack of papers seems a little less daunting when we vary our style of responding. Sometimes we need to vary our approach because we realize that a particular student or a particular assignment demands a different method. And sometimes we just need to experiment with different approaches to make responding more interesting and creative. Here are a few methods to vary the rhythm and style of responding:

- **Face-to-face conferences:** Conferences provide an opportunity for one-on-one instruction and allow us to get to know our students better. Of course, such meetings also allow students to get to know us better as teachers. Conferences save time, too. Rather than spending twenty minutes writing a comment about a murky draft that might sound like a series of contingencies—*If your purpose is X, you might want to try this approach, but if your purpose is Y, you might want to try this other approach*—I can turn to a student and ask: *What do you want to say in your paper?* And rather than writing lengthy explanations about how to formulate a thesis or how to state the main point of a paragraph in a topic sentence, I can personally teach these elements, one lesson at a time. Over the years, I've learned that face-to-face conferences work best when students do most of the talking, take notes during the meeting, and leave the conference with a solid plan and a sense of confidence about their next step.

- **Recorded oral comments:** Most teachers find it impossible to schedule face-to-face meetings with each student for each assignment, but it is possible, given the range of technologies—audiovisual screen captures, inserted oral commentary in electronic drafts, MP3 files— to offer oral comments to each student. Many students find the familiar, encouraging tone of their teachers' voices to be an easier method for receiving comments. And many teachers find that they are able to offer students more detailed explanations by speaking their responses.

- **Podcasts:** Here's a variation of the "Trends and Patterns" handout: Record a podcast about one particular rhetorical or grammatical element for the entire class. For instance, if I notice a pattern across all students' drafts—lack of transitions or missing signal phrases— I might record a three-minute podcast to provide a fuller, more detailed explanation than can be given in written or oral comments. Podcasts can be mini-lessons, available on the class Web site for multiple listening sessions, using examples from students' drafts to illustrate lessons, and extending a teacher's voice beyond the classroom walls.

Mentoring students to become thoughtful readers

Mentoring students to become thoughtful and critical readers not only shares the work of responding but also, and more importantly, creates a vibrant classroom community. Electronic resources—discussion boards or e-mail—make it even easier for peers to offer responses throughout the writing process. The more students read of one another's work, the more they learn; the more they learn, the better they write. Yet students need guidance to become thoughtful readers and responders, just as their teachers do. And students need to see the benefits derived from listening to and learning from their classmates.

One of my goals in the first two weeks of a semester is to build and sustain a vibrant writing community by modeling for students how to give and receive respectful, meaningful responses. I strive to move students away from emotional statements—liking or disliking their peers' drafts—and to move them away from thinking of a draft as a broken-down car needing repairs. Instead, in peer groups, I ask students to read a draft and discuss what revision strategies they would offer. And I ask them, as a group, to draft their own "manifesto" about the kind of comments they want to receive from their peers. See page 14 for a sample student statement about feedback. At some point in the middle of the semester, we check in as a community to see if the manifesto still guides peer response, or if it requires revision to evolve with students' growing authority as readers and responders.

One of my favorite peer group activities is to ask students to create their own "Trends and Patterns" handout or podcast for the class. After reading and responding to their peers' drafts, they are charged with the analytical task of identifying three or four patterns of common rhetorical and grammatical problems. Their handout or podcast identifies the problems, provides illustrations of it, and indicates where in their handbook students can turn for instruction and advice.

Resisting the urge to correct grammar and punctuation errors

Conversations about the paper load inevitably find their way to thorny questions about grammar and punctuation errors. To ignore such errors, especially ones that impede communication, sends the wrong signal to students. Yet to mark and correct each error sends an equally wrong and discouraging signal. But where is the middle ground to balance instruction with response?

We need to remind ourselves that errors are a natural and normal part of learning to write. As composition teachers, we have a wide repertoire of strategies to employ when teaching grammar and punctuation, including lessons and exercises, in class or online. Correcting students' errors is one such strategy, but it is not always the most effective. When teachers become their students' copy editors, they take away the responsibility and opportunity for students to recognize and resolve their own mistakes. Research studies have shown that students can identify and correct their own errors, if given the opportunity.[3]

We can and should expect students to proofread, to use their handbooks, to go to the writing center, and to seek help from their teachers to answer specific grammar or punctuation questions. And we must feel we are able to hold students accountable, even if we haven't pointed out every error in their drafts. Holding students accountable not only promotes learning but also teaches them to use resources and be active participants in their own learning.

It is often difficult, though, to resist correcting students' grammatical and punctuation errors. After all, as writing teachers we are trained to recognize and remedy such errors. And it is often difficult to resist students' expectations that we mark all their errors. Yet I've found that using a similar responding strategy for grammar and punctuation errors as for rhetorical problems saves time and increases students' responsibility and authority. That is, I focus on patterns—an overuse of passives or misuse of apostrophes, for example—rather than correcting each and every mistake. Similarly, spending classroom time at the beginning of the semester to explain my typical approach—what language and format I'll use to respond to grammatical and punctuation errors, including abbreviations or shorthand—helps students learn from such comments.

Asking students to become their own copy editors encourages them to develop a reflective and analytical habit of mind. And it frees teachers from being comma cops. Instead of correcting each error, I circle, highlight, or underline a pattern of errors or put a check mark in the margins to indicate the presence of an error. It is the students' responsibility to find the remaining errors of the same type. And instead of rewriting their sentences, I make suggestions: *How about using active verbs instead of* be *verbs?* The specific choice of active verbs is theirs, not mine, and they learn more from the process than if I had chosen one for them.

To strengthen their writing skills, I ask students to keep editing logs in which they copy and edit their sentences, write the grammar or punctuation rules, and explain how to correct the errors. Editing logs are a variation on the theme of "trends and patterns." When students identify *their* pattern of errors, apply principles from the handbook, and chart their own progress, they gain control over their writing. The goal is to keep the focus on learning and on building skills, one lesson at a time.

---

[3] Richard Haswell found that students could identify 61.1 percent of their errors on their own. See Richard Haswell, "Minimal Marking," *College English* 45.6 (1983): 600–04.

Finding a role for grading rubrics

In a book dedicated to the power of comments to shape students' writing, it might seem counterintuitive to include a section on rubrics, seemingly impersonal tools, which are often the antithesis of a teacher's voice. Yet the problem is not the rubric itself; the problem is that it is too often misused, especially when it replaces commentary and exists as the only response students receive—numbers and check marks—instead of words crafted *to* a student. Rubrics are an important part of a teacher's toolbox and can help manage the paper load and ease the burden of grading. Very few teachers enjoy grading, but the task becomes less overwhelming with clear assessment criteria. (For a sample rubric, see page 35.)

Whenever I see a rubric, I want to know its role in instruction: Are the elements within a rubric specific to the assignment? Does the language of the rubric form the basis of instruction around the assignment? Does the rubric clarify expectations and assignment goals? If so, a rubric is a useful method to focus comments, avoid subjectivity, and provide large-scale assessments across a class and an entire writing program.

As the Columbus State University writing center tutors suggest, we need to discuss the rubric in class, use it to inform the writing process, and let students learn from it, but we shouldn't use it to justify grades. Rubrics take away the mystery of grades and say to students: *Here are the goals of the assignment and the criteria used to evaluate your papers. Your writing is measured against these criteria. Learn from them.*

6

A case study:
One reader reading

Throughout this book, I have suggested that responding is rooted in a partnership between students and teachers and, as in any relationship, develops its own language and meaning. Part of the quid pro quo of any relationship is the reciprocity of giving and receiving advice. What advice might students give their teachers about responding, I wondered, if given the opportunity? So I posed this simple question to the Bunker Hill Community College students I interviewed: "What suggestions would you offer your teachers to help them give more effective comments?"

The Bunker Hill students' responses are straightforward and direct, specific and earnest, and they come from their desire to have their writing read as communication, not as a collection of mistakes. Here is a sampling of the thoughtful advice offered by Bunker Hill students:

> On the first day of class, teachers should tell their students: Comments are
> to help you learn. Here is why I comment; here is how I comment. Welcome to
> my class!

> Give something positive before taking something away. Give the sweet before
> the sour.

> Fixing isn't learning. Give us suggestions to help us learn.

> Write comments that begin conversations, not end them.

> Provoke us. Help us think for ourselves.

> Encourage us. Show us how to become stronger writers.

In this final chapter, I use the Bunker Hill students' advice to guide my reading and responses to one student writer, Lena Santos, whose draft appears on pages 37–40. I offer my responses not as a definitive set of comments but as one reader reading — a reader who wants to begin a conversation to help Lena become a stronger writer.

Reprinted here are Lena's assignment; a rubric for the assignment; her Dear Reader letter; her first draft, with my marginal and end comments; and my reflections about reading Lena's draft.

Sample composition assignment and accompanying rubric

ESSAY ASSIGNMENT #2: ANALYZING VISUAL TEXTS

For this assignment, you will focus on a contemporary problem and analyze how that problem is addressed through the rhetoric of visual texts—photographs, advertisements, cartoons, and so on. You'll be asking yourself two key questions: How do various images present different perspectives or angles of vision on the problem? What do the authors of these visual texts want the audience to think and do about the problem?

Step 1: Select two visual texts to analyze. Look for texts that use different rhetorical strategies to accomplish their purposes. Comparing and contrasting these texts is part of what you'll do, so select your texts with that in mind.

Step 2: Identify a question, a problem, or an issue to address.

Step 3: Analyze the commonalities and differences of your chosen texts through the lens of the question, problem, or issue you have identified.

Step 4: Write a 500-to-1,000-word essay, double-spaced, MLA formatted, plus works cited. Draft and Dear Reader letter due September 28.

RUBRIC FOR ESSAY ASSIGNMENT #2: ANALYZING VISUAL TEXTS

Writer:	
CRITERIA	**INSTRUCTOR'S NOTES**
The writer uses the introduction to ask a provocative, analytical question or to identify a problem.	
The writer develops a clear, debatable thesis that sets up an academic analysis.	
The writer explores commonalities and differences between selected texts.	
The writer refers to specific details in the texts to support the thesis.	
The writer follows MLA format and includes a works cited page.	
The writer submits a carefully edited essay on October 8.	

Sample Dear Reader letter

Dear Reader:

This is the first time I have been asked to write a paper about visual texts. Before writing this draft, I never thought about the fact that a photograph might be sending a message or making a social statement. The strengths of my paper are the photographs I chose because they are such sad, heartbreaking photos.

The thesis of my paper is "there are many similarities and differences between the two photographs." I would like my reader to tell me if I do a fair job showing these similarities and differences. Also, please let me know how to improve my writing.

If I had two more days to work on this draft, I would try to do a better job explaining the message of these photos.

Lena Santos

Sample first draft with comments

Santos 1

good title:
try to connect
your title to
the problem
you are
analyzing.
What problem
is posed by
children
smoking?

State the
problem
in your
introduction
to hook your
readers.

Lena Santos

Professor Sommers

English 101

28 September 2011

From Cradles to Cigarettes

Every day of our lives we pass billboards, read magazines, watch television, but we never really think in depth about what the visual text is actually saying. By not truly analyzing visual texts, you end up being manipulated by what a photographer is telling you to do. If you take the time to sit down and really analyze what is in front of you, you can really receive a much stronger message than just glancing at it.

When comparing two visual texts, I chose two photographs, which involve the illustration of children who are smoking cigarettes. The first one is titled *Amanda and Her Cousin Amy* and features a young girl with a cigarette in her hand. The second one, *New Year's Eve*, is of a five-year-old French boy who is smoking a cigarette on New Year's Eve with his father blessing his head as he smokes. When comparing the two texts, a viewer sees many similarities and differences between the two photographs.

Fig. 1 This photograph was staged so that the artist could tell a story. (Mark.)

Santos 2

Fig. 2   This photograph suggests that what might be taboo in the United States is customary elsewhere. (Denzel.)

What story is each photograph telling?

Great observation. Why does it matter if a photo is staged? Does a photo tell a different story if it is staged?

Taboo — an interesting word! What is taboo about a father blessing his son for smoking?

When it comes to the way the photographs were taken, the two differ greatly. The picture of the young girl was staged in order to tell a story. However, the photograph of the five-year-old boy was not staged and was a still frame of an actual situation. The context in which both of these pictures were taken evokes different emotions. Knowing that the picture of the young girl was actually a staged photograph makes you feel somewhat relieved that smoking cigarettes is perhaps not an everyday activity for her. Also, it makes you think about what the photographer was trying to get across by taking such a picture. When it comes to the young boy smoking a cigarette and knowing that the situation is in fact real, it evokes a kind of sadness for the viewer. Knowing this child is only five years old and is already damaging his lungs is hard enough to imagine, let alone seeing his father encourage it. In the United States, a child smoking is somewhat taboo. Knowing this young boy could end up with lung cancer at an incredibly early age breaks your heart.

A difference between the two visual texts is the actual content in the images. In the photograph of the little girl, there is no parent present. No one is approving her activity. In fact, it seems as if she is breaking

Santos 3

the rules with her makeup and her jewelry, too. The boy is smoking a
real cigarette in the presence of his father, who seems to approve of
the behavior. The boy is not portrayed as rebellious at all, but actually
obedient. The image of the boy with a cigarette pressed to his lips
suggests to the reader how different customs are in certain countries.
Also, knowing the detrimental effects of cigarettes and how they contain
carcinogens breaks the viewer's heart. Knowing that the child in the
picture is permanently damaging his lungs at such a tender age is very
difficult to look at.

A similarity between the two pictures is the use of black and white.
The photographer of *Amanda and Her Cousin Amy* most likely chose black
and white to gain focus on the girl in the picture as opposed to her
surroundings. In the photo of the young boy, the black and white colors
draw attention to the child smoking. The older businessman (and assumed
father), with his hand blessing the boy's head, is dressed in black with a
bright white shirt underneath. The young boy is dressed in shades of black
and gray, wearing a leather jacket and tie, which draws attention to him in
the same way the white pool and plainly dressed cousin draws attention to
the girl. The use of contrast in these two photographs focuses the viewer's
gaze to what they are intended to look at.

All in all, I believe the photographers of both images did a great job
at using various techniques to send their messages. Before writing this
essay, I have to honestly say that I would glance at advertisements and
photographs in magazines or on television and not think twice. Looking
carefully at photographs helps a viewer to go in depth and get more
meaning from them.

Good observations and details in this paragraph. Revise your essay to include more of this level of detail.

Santos 4

Works Cited

Denzel, Jesco. *St. Jacques Gypsy Boy on New Year's Eve*. *VervePhoto*. Geoffrey Hiller,
     2008. Web. 26 Sep. 2011.

Mark, Mary Ellen. *Amanda and Her Cousin Amy, North Carolina, 1990*.
     Mary Ellen Mark: 25 Years. Ed. Marianne Fulton. Boston: Bulfinch, 1991.
     107. Print.

Comment [NancySommers2]: Dear Lena:
You have selected two powerful photos for your analysis. Now push
your own good thinking to ask yourself: Why are these photos so
sad and heartbreaking? What problem do they illustrate? You hint
at a problem by using the word *taboo*, an evocative word. Do both
photographs tell the same story? If not, what competing stories
do they tell? And how do the photos work together (compare and
contrast) to deepen our understanding of the problem?
Here are some strategies to help you approach your next draft:
- Start by returning to the photos and rereading them. Try asking
  some questions about these photos that you don't have answers
  to. You've started this process already by asking about the
  "staged" quality of one of the photos. Does it matter to a viewer if
  the photograph is staged? If so, why or how?
- Revise your introduction to set up your analysis. Your thesis needs
  to be more than a statement of fact — the existence of similarities
  and differences — and needs to have what we call in class "an
  argumentative edge." See the "Trends and Patterns" handout for
  more suggestions about revising your introduction and setting up
  your analysis.
I look forward to reading your next draft.

Nancy Sommers

Reading Lena's draft

Lena's assignment invites her into the academy, asks her to do serious work,
and then gives her the freedom to select images and define her own interests. Her challenge in writing this first draft is to find an entry point—a
question, a problem, a hook for her analysis—and to use this entry point to
organize her comparative analysis. If students such as Lena have difficulty
writing about a single text, they will have even greater challenges when

asked to bring two texts into conversation with each other. And if they can't find an entry point, they will be writing essays that are structured as lists, or as a back-and-forth ping-pong game of similarities and differences, rather than as a sustained, focused analysis.

As a reader, I also need an entry point—a hook or a thesis—to organize my comments and to give Lena my scale of concerns. It would be easy to overwhelm Lena by pointing out all the limitations of her draft and cataloging her mistakes, but such comments would, in the words of the Bunker Hill students, "end conversations" and "take something away" without helping her learn how to become a stronger writer. This is the second assignment in her college writing class, and she still has eight more weeks to build on her own strengths and consolidate her gains.

So how do I begin a conversation? One way is to focus on the "sweet before the sour," by showing her the significant strengths of her first draft. Lena is trying out the voice and style of academic analysis, even if she isn't sure how to proceed, and is trying hard to figure out what it means to "read" a photograph. I want to show Lena how to build on these strengths, especially how to transform her observations into analysis, while also giving her a realistic picture of how she is, or isn't, meeting the assignment's goals.

The most important lesson to teach Lena is how to launch her comparative analysis, especially how to move beyond reporting similarities and differences as if they were ends rather than the means to analysis. To do so, she needs to establish an overarching frame for her analysis by figuring out the conversation between the photos. How does one photo extend, complicate, contradict, or illuminate the other? What are the grounds for comparing these two photos? And what problem or puzzle do these photos comment on?

One of the great intellectual leaps of first-year writing is the move from summary to analysis, from reporting to interpreting, which is one of the reasons we find ourselves so frequently commenting *Summarize less, analyze more.* And Lena shows us that she is still struggling to move from summary—"here's what I see and notice"—to analysis—"here's what it means and why it matters." But she is moving in the right direction by thinking about the "story" of each photo and pointing out the "taboo" aspect of a father blessing his son for smoking or a photographer's provocative "staging" a photo of a girl smoking.

Following the advice of the Bunker Hill students, I would tell Lena and her classmates that my comments are intended to help them learn. I am an overcommenter, so I need to remind myself not to comment on everything that I notice. I chose not to comment on Lena's wordy sentences, vague language, or comma errors because I want her to focus on global concerns, rethinking her entire draft, rather than fixing words or sentences that would best be deleted. If these problems continue in the revised draft, I'll follow the "minimal marking" method and ask her to focus on them in her editing log.

Reading Lena's draft reminds me of the pleasures of responding to student writers—a sacred trust given to writing teachers—and of the patience and humility that are required for our work. As a profession, we are defined by our belief that writing is learning, and we are characterized by the paper load we carry with us, in our backpacks or briefcases, or on our laptops or desktops.

Lena's first draft is a brave attempt to do something she's never done before—read and analyze visual texts—and as a reader I want to show her that it is within her grasp to do something different in the next draft. I want her to read my comments and say: "This is something I can do." And as a writer, Lena gives us plenty of evidence that she's ready to do so.

Brief Bibliography

A rich and abundant literature exists on the topic of responding to student writers. Here are some important works that I return to for instruction and guidance.

Anson, Chris M. "Response Styles and Ways of Knowing." *Writing and Response: Theory, Practice, and Research.* Ed. Chris Anson. Urbana: NCTE, 1989. 332–66. Print.

Brannon, Lil, and C. H. Knoblauch. "On Students' Rights to Their Own Texts: A Model of Teacher Response." *College Composition and Communication* 33 (1982): 157–66. Print.

Elbow, Peter. *Writing without Teachers.* New York: Oxford University Press, 1973. Print.

Haswell, Richard. "Minimal Marking." *College English* 45.6 (1983): 600–04. Print.

Lee, Melanie. "Rhetorical Roulette: Does Writing Faculty Overload Disable Effective Response to Student Writing?" *Teaching English in the Two-Year College* 37 (2009): 165–77. Print.

Sommers, Jeff. "Spoken Response: Space, Time, and Movies of the Mind." *Writing with Elbow.* Ed. P. Belanoff, M. Dickson, S. Fontaine, and C. Moran. Logan: Utah State University Press, 2002. 172–86. Print.

Straub, Richard, ed. *Key Works on Teacher Response: An Anthology.* Portsmouth: Boynton/Cook, 2006. Print.

Straub, Richard, and Ronald Lunsford, eds. *Twelve Readers Reading: Responding to College Student Writing.* Cresskill: Hampton Press, 1995. Print.

White, E. M. "Post-structural Literary Criticism and the Response to Student Writing." *College Composition and Communication* 35 (1984): 186–95. Print.

Yancey, Kathleen Blake. *Reflection in the Writing Classroom.* Logan: Utah State University Press, 1998. Print.

Responding to student writers: Best practices

Preparing to respond

- **Be positive.** The goal of commenting is to offer encouragement and honest assessment. Look for strengths and help students build on those strengths.
- **Start a conversation.** Think of responding as teaching, not correcting — especially in early drafts. Responding is most fruitful for students when you engage them in a dialogue.
- **Share models.** Share with students a rough draft and the final draft of the same paper. Let them see that true revising is often a renovation project rather than just patchwork and fixes.
- **Discuss the purpose of comments.** Spend class time talking with students about comments. Introduce them to the types of comments you give, and explain any symbols or shorthand you use.

Responding to rough drafts

- **Go global.** Resist asking students to patch and edit before they develop their ideas. Asking students to think about grammar, punctuation, and word choice in sentences that may not make it to the next draft could be a waste of your time and theirs.
- **Know when to go local.** In a rough draft, you might identify patterns of sentence-level, or local, errors instead of marking individual errors. Identifying patterns — representative strengths and limitations — helps students gain control over their writing and saves you time.
- **Continue the lesson.** Responding is more effective when the language of comments grows from discussions in the classroom. Students shouldn't be encountering terms or ideas for the first time in the margins of their papers.
- **Teach one lesson at a time.** Reading an entire draft, quickly, before commenting may actually save time. Ask: What single lesson (or two) do I want to teach here? And how will my comments teach this lesson? Avoid overcommenting: An individual writer can learn only a finite set of lessons when revising a single paper.

Encouraging revision

- **Tread purposefully and lightly.** Avoid leaving too heavy a footprint in the margins of students' papers. Use your comments to show students how to start revising without suggesting specific language for the revision.
- **Foster reflection.** Ask students to submit a cover letter or a Dear Reader letter along with a rough draft. Such a letter reminds students that they are writing for a reader, allows them to begin a dialogue about their work, and provides an opportunity for them to articulate any concerns about their draft.
- **Require a revision plan.** When you hand back drafts with your comments, assign students to review the comments, perhaps during the final fifteen minutes of a class, and to write a one-page revision plan in which they explain what they learned from the comments and how they plan to use the comments as they revise.

Responding to final drafts

- **Refresh your memory.** Before responding to final drafts, reread the assignment and the expectations you may have listed for students. Doing so keeps the commentary tied to the assignment.
- **Put final comments in context.** On a final draft, evaluate the strengths and limitations in the context of the assignment's goals. Responding is far easier when the goals of an assignment have shaped the language and lessons that prepared students for the assignment.
- **Provide a bridge.** Writers develop their skills over time. It's too much to expect that first-year writing teachers can cover every lesson students need in order to write successfully across the curriculum. Make sure your comments on final drafts do double duty. Final comments can evaluate success in relation to the specific assignment, but they should also provide a bridge — a transportable lesson — to the next assignment or to assignments in other courses.

Index